COOKING WITH MATH!

MAKING PASTA WITH MATH!

By Santana Hunt

Gareth Stevens PUBLISHING

leveled reader math

Please visit our website, www.garethstevens.com. For a free color catalog of all our high-quality books, call toll free 1-800-542-2595 or fax 1-877-542-2596.

Cataloging-in-Publication Data

Names: Hunt, Santana.
Title: Making pasta with math! / Santana Hunt.
Description: New York : Gareth Stevens Publishing, 2020. | Series: Cooking with math! | Includes glossary and index.
Identifiers: ISBN 9781538245576 (pbk.) | ISBN 9781538245590 (library bound) | ISBN 9781538245583 (6 pack)
Subjects: LCSH: Mathematics–Juvenile literature. | Cooking–Juvenile literature. | Cooking (Pasta)–Juvenile literature. | Pasta products–Juvenile literature.
Classification: LCC QA40.5 H86 2020 | DDC 510–dc23

Published in 2020 by
Gareth Stevens Publishing
111 East 14th Street, Suite 349
New York, NY 10003

Designer: Katelyn E. Reynolds
Editor: Kate Mikoley

Photo credits: Cover, p. 1 Francesco83/Shutterstock.com; pp. 1–24 (gingham background) Mika Besfamilnaya/Shutterstock.com; pp. 1–24 (recipe background) A. Zhuravleva/Shutterstock.com; p. 5 (spaghetti, elbow macaroni, and penne) Marisa Lia/Shutterstock.com; p. 5 (lasagna noodles) Fotos593/Shutterstock.com; p. 7 Steve Cukrov/Shutterstock.com; p. 8 Yellow Cat/Shutterstock.com; p. 11 designs by Jack/Shutterstock.com; p. 15 Elena Veselova/Shutterstock.com; p. 16 Vladimir Wrangel/Shutterstock.com; p. 19 Julia Mikhaylova/Shutterstock.com.

Printed in the United States of America

CPSIA compliance information: Batch #CW20GS: For further information contact Gareth Stevens, New York, New York at 1-800-542-2595.

CONTENTS

Boldface words appear in the glossary.

Time to Cook!

Whether you call your dinner pasta, macaroni, or noodles, it's sure to taste good! You can use math to help make it yummy. Measuring, subtraction, telling time, addition, and multiplication are just some of the skills you may use to make a great pasta plate!

Ask an adult before using the stove or oven!

Homemade Spaghetti Sauce

Recipes list what **ingredients** are needed to make a dish. They tell how much of each ingredient to use too. Recipes use measurements such as cups and tablespoons. They may also use pounds or **ounces**, measurements commonly found on jars, cans, and boxes.

Today, our
special flour blend
ensures that RONZONI
pasta is...
• Always Firm
• Never Sticky
• Simply Delicious
We guarantee it!
Simply Perfect Pasta
Ronzoni Sono Buoni...
Ronzoni is So Good!®
A low fat, sodium free,
cholesterol free food.
Rotini
Serving Suggestion
ENRICHED
MACARONI
NET WT. 1 LB. (454 g)

The recipe calls for 16 ounces of spaghetti. You have an 8-ounce box of spaghetti. How many more ounces of spaghetti do you need? Check your answer on page 22!

$$
\begin{array}{r}
16 \text{ ounces} \\
- \ 8 \text{ ounces} \\
\hline
? \text{ ounces of spaghetti}
\end{array}
$$

HOMEMADE SPAGHETTI SAUCE

Ingredients:

2 tablespoons olive oil
2 cloves garlic, chopped small
one can diced plum tomatoes (about 28 ounces)
a pinch of salt and pepper
one 16-ounce box of spaghetti

Instructions:

1. With an adult's help, heat olive oil in a large frying pan. Add garlic and cook until just brown.

2. Mix in tomatoes, salt, and pepper. Bring to a **simmer** and cook for about 30 minutes.

3. Use a spoon to break up any tomatoes that haven't fallen apart.

4. Prepare spaghetti by following the box directions.

5. Spoon sauce over cooked pasta.

Easy Macaroni and Cheese

Sometimes, a recipe tells you about how long it will take to make. It often says how long some of the steps will take too. It may list a **range** of time a step may take, such as 12 to 15 minutes.

The box of macaroni says it takes about 12 minutes to make. Step two of this recipe says it takes about 5 minutes. Step three also takes about 5 minutes. How long will you be cooking?

$$\begin{array}{r} 12 \text{ minutes} \\ 5 \text{ minutes} \\ + \ 5 \text{ minutes} \\ \hline ? \text{ minutes} \end{array}$$

EASY
MACARONI AND CHEESE

Ingredients:

one 16-ounce box elbow macaroni
4 cups milk
4 cups shredded cheddar cheese
1/2 cup butter
1/2 cup flour
1 teaspoon salt

Instructions:

1. Prepare pasta by following the box directions.
2. In a large saucepan, melt the butter. Stir in flour and salt and mix for about 5 minutes.
3. Pour in milk and stir for another 5 minutes until bubbling.
4. Mix in cheddar cheese until melted.
5. Pour cheese over macaroni and stir.

Cheesy Lasagna

Pasta is a great meal to make for families because a box of it doesn't cost very much! In fact, a box of pasta can cost less than a dollar. Special pastas, such as those made from whole wheat flour, commonly cost more.

Boxes of lasagna noodles are on sale at the store for 65¢ each. When you're ready to pay, you have 3 pennies, 1 nickel, 2 dimes, and 3 quarters. Which coins will you use to pay exactly 65¢?

CHEESY LASAGNA

Ingredients:

9 uncooked lasagna noodles
2 1/2 cups shredded mozzarella cheese
2 cups ricotta cheese
2 eggs
one jar tomato sauce (about 24 ounces)
1/3 cup grated Parmesan cheese
1 tablespoon Italian seasoning
1 teaspoon garlic powder

Instructions:

1. Heat oven to 350°F (177°C). Lightly beat eggs and mix with 2 cups of mozzarella cheese, ricotta cheese, Italian seasoning, and garlic powder.
2. Pour about 1 cup of sauce into the bottom of a 9 X 13-inch (23 X 33 cm) pan. Place three lasagna noodles on top. Spoon half of the cheese mixture on top. Redo this step.
3. Top with the last three noodles, sauce, mozzarella cheese, and the Parmesan cheese.
4. Cover pan with foil. Bake for about 45 minutes. Remove foil and bake 10 to 15 more minutes.

Cold Pesto Salad

Recipes help us learn to cook. But they're just a guide! You can make many pasta dishes your own by adding more of the ingredients you like. Or, you may decide to use different ingredients based on what you already have at home!

This recipe would be great with broccoli in it too! If you use twice as much broccoli as cherry tomatoes, how many cups of broccoli would you use?

$$\begin{array}{r} 2 \text{ cups} \\ \times\ 2 \\ \hline ? \text{ cups of broccoli} \end{array}$$

COLD PESTO SALAD

Ingredients:

one 16-ounce box penne pasta
one jar **pesto** (about 6 ounces)
2 cups cherry tomatoes, cut in half
2 cups mini mozzarella balls

Instructions:

1. Prepare the pasta by following the box directions.
2. **Drain** pasta and allow to cool completely.
3. Mix in pesto, tomatoes, and mozzarella balls.
4. Put in the refrigerator for at least an hour before serving.

Glossary

drain: to get rid of liquid by letting it flow out

ingredient: a food that is mixed with other foods

ounce: a unit of weight equal to 1/16 of a pound. A fluid ounce measures liquids and equals 1/16 of a pint.

pesto: a sauce made with basil

range: a series of numbers that includes the highest and lowest amounts possible

recipe: an explanation of how to make food

simmer: to cook something until almost boiling for a time

Answer Key

p. 8 8 ounces

p. 12 22 minutes

p. 16 2 quarters, 1 dime, 1 nickel

p. 20 4 cups

For More Information

Books

Canavan, Thomas. *Math Is Awesome!: 101 Incredible Things Every Kid Should Know*. London, UK: Arcturus, 2018.

Gilbert, Sara. *Italian Food*. Mankato, MN: Creative Education, 2015.

Websites

2nd Grade Math

www.mathplayground.com/grade_2_games.html
Find math games here!

Recipes & Cooking for Kids

kidshealth.org/en/kids/recipes/
Discover more recipes you can make on this website.

Publisher's note to educators and parents: Our editors have carefully reviewed these websites to ensure that they are suitable for students. Many websites change frequently, however, and we cannot guarantee that a site's future contents will continue to meet our high standards of quality and educational value. Be advised that students should be closely supervised whenever they access the internet.

Index